What are THESE?

and what is THAT?

by Beck Haga

This book belongs to

_____

What are
THESE?

and what is
THAT?

written + illustrated
by Beck Haga

What are THESE?

a touch

a breeze

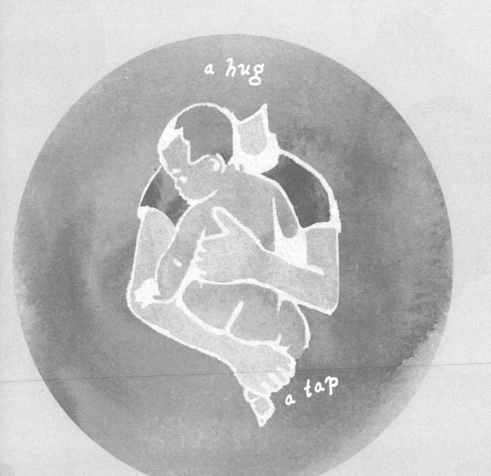

What is this?
What are those?

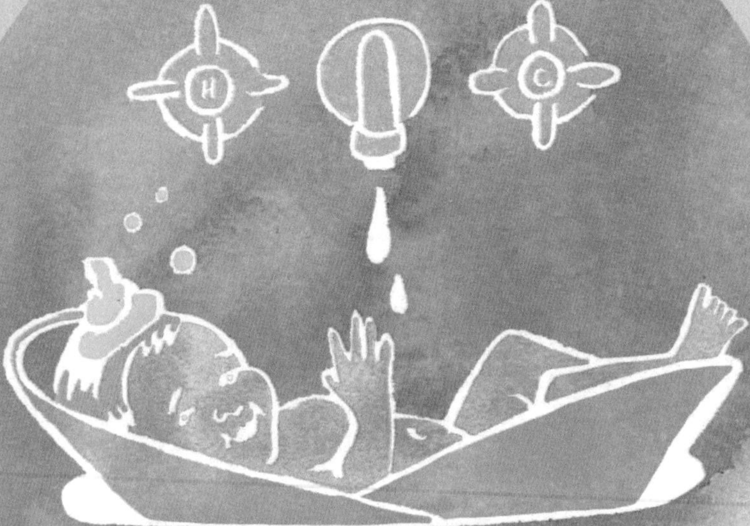

a baby bath

a change of clothes

What is that?
What is this?

a furry cat

What is this?
What are those?

a teddy bear

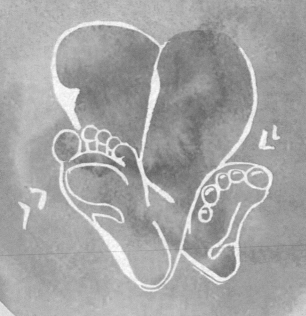

some tickled toes

I like it when you
move us slow

So I can feel and
start to know

So I can watch,
so I can see

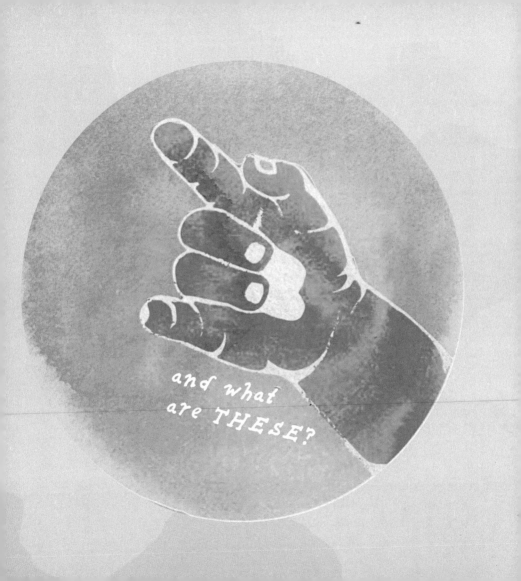

All about
"What are These? and What is That?"

Recommended for 4 months +

Reading to newborns is highly recommended however, they can't see in color just yet...

This happy little book celebrates baby's first observations of the world around them as their senses begin to develop.

Did you know that a newborn child has already made sensory memories (tactile, auditory and visual) during their prenatal life? It is comforting for baby to experience these familiar senses during their first weeks and months of life alongside introductions to new sensory stimulation.

This book encourages adults to gently speak to baby about each new stimulation with the questions,
"What are these? What is that?"

Reading to and narrating everyday experience to babies and young children is so important! It provides the building blocks for language. And it gives them the tools for forming lifelong social and emotional skills –not to mention helps form bonds between baby and their caregivers.

Asking questions about experiences and allowing one another to reflect and communicate will be one of the most valuable resources for your child as they grow!

Following your child's development, and the Montessori Method, this book will serve as a great tool to bond with your child and encourage you to cherish your new routine.

The illustrations are recommended for use as visual stimulus during tummy time as well!

Understanding your Baby

Exploration

Babies are the greatest natural explorers. As they look at things, taste them, smell them, touch them, swing them around, and toss them in the air, they are coming to understand all of these sensations for the very first time. As parents and caregivers, we can provide our children with things to explore, give them time to explore freely, make the environment safe for independent exploration and allow opportunities for hands-on learning.

Repetition

We all learn through repetition - doing something new over and over again until, finally, after much practice (and a whole lot of failure), we figure it out! Repetition leads to mastery. This process of trial and error is an innate human tendency.

Oftentimes adults mistake this repetition as a sign of struggle and a call for help. When we see our children repeating an action, it is important that we take a step back and allow them the opportunity to grow.

With these tendencies in mind, it is a wonderful idea to sprinkle our children's days with reading familiar stories, singing beloved songs, and creating a routine that suits our family!

Language

From our baby's earliest days, we may notice their interest in reaching for and watching our mouths as we speak. As our baby reaches 3 to 6 months, we may notice that this interest has turned into a fascination – one in which we find our little one focusing intently at our mouths and faces with unblinking eyes while we speak.

It is at this moment that our child is ready to engage in their own form of conversation and to build a strong foundation of language. We can encourage our child's language development through engaging in "baby talk" by repeating the sounds they make back to them as if in conversation. We can also speak to our baby in a sing–song tone and use our hands and facial expressions while narrating the activities of the day... "Now it's time to go for a walk! Then we'll go home and read our favorite book."

TERAKOYA LEARNING IS AN EDUCATIONAL RESOURCE COMPANY.

WE CREATE IDEAS THAT ENCOURAGE THE DISCOVERY OF JOY IN LEARNING.

TEACHER MADE IN ALAMEDA, CA – USA

Following the principles of Montessori educational philosophy, we provide classes, events, printed and digital learning materials as well as handmade educational goods for children and their parents.

TERAKOYALEARNING@GMAIL.COM

TERAKOYALEARNING.SQUARE.SITE

@TERAKOYAKIDS

Made in the USA
Las Vegas, NV
06 December 2024

13466859R00017